Lesley Waters studied French Cuisine for three years at Ealing College, which included time as a chef at the Waldorf Hotel. In 1978 she joined Prue Leith's Restaurant and was quickly promoted to the position of senior chef. She later joined Leith's School of Food and Wine as an instructor, rising to head teacher, and she often represented British food at international cookery displays, taking as her theme 'good food for health's sake'. Lesley Waters has worked in television since 1989. In addition to 'GMTV' and 'Bazaar' her work has included writing and presenting a series of cookery programmes, teaming up with Malcolm Gluck to present the 'Superplonk' video and co-presenting a 12-part series about healthy living. During 1996 she was one of the main presenters of 'Can't Cook Won't Cook', and she is currently part of the teams on 'Ready Steady Cook' and 'Mixing It' for the BBC and Channel 5.

Lesley Waters' previous books include *Bazaar Hearty Eater*, *Fifteen Minute Feasts*, *Sainsbury's Quick and Easy Food for Friends* and *Weight Watchers Carefree Christmas*.

Also available in Orion paperback

APPLES & PEARS
Gloria Thomas

AROUSING AROMAS
Kay Cooper

EAT SAFELY
Janet Wright

HEALTH SPA AT HOME
Josephine Fairley

SPRING CLEAN YOUR SYSTEM
Jane Garton

JUICE UP YOUR ENERGY LEVELS

LESLEY WATERS

ORION

An Orion Paperback
First published in Great Britain in 1998 by
Orion Books Ltd,
Orion House, 5 Upper St Martin's Lane,
London WC2H 9EA

A CIP catalogue record for this book
is available from the British Library.

ISBN: 0 75281 602 0

Printed and bound in Great Britain by
The Guernsey Press Co. Ltd., Guernsey, C.I.

CONTENTS

INTRODUCTION

The pace of life is becoming more and more hectic. Finding the time to cook a meal or even drink enough fluid can be difficult and they are often replaced by yet another chocolate bar or sugar-laden fizzy drink to keep us going throughout the day.

Our bodies are not built to perform well on this type of empty fuel, so we get tired and hungry and end up cooking or drinking something quick and not very nutritious. So the vicious circle continues – but it doesn't have to.

Fruit and vegetables are an important part of our daily diet and it is vital that we eat enough of them. They not only taste good, but, when combined with a nutritious, balanced diet, have great energising qualities.

Perhaps at one time or another the idea of fresh fruit and vegetable juices has appealed to you, but in reality making and drinking a glass of carrot or orange juice, or investing in an expensive juicer, has not really tempted you. You may only be able to name a few fruits that can be juiced – probably orange, grapefruit or tomato – but in fact the combinations of fruits and vegetables are endless. Juices are exciting, thirst quenching, exhilarating and quick and easy to prepare. You don't even need a specialised juicer! Seven of the eight chapters in this book will only require a trusty liquidiser or food processor. *Juice Up Your Energy Levels* will help you to discover a whole new approach to juicing.

This book covers an array of food juices with an exciting collection of recipes that can be incorporated into everyday living. There are seven 'juicy' chapters, from 'Just for Kicks', recipes for beginner's juices, to 'Souper Smoothies' for more filling food juices and even 'Juicy Dressings' to liven up your salad days, and 'Flash Juices' for jazzing up carton juices. For special occasions, there are fun chapters packed with punches for parties and glamorous cocktails for the evening hour.

By the time you've tasted your way through these seven chapters you'll probably be hooked! You may even be ready to invest in the ultimate juice equipment. The final chapter 'Nuts and Bolts' provides a selection of more concentrated juice recipes suitable for the automatic juicing machine.

So what do you need in your kitchen for juicing if you haven't invested in an electric juicer? Chapter One gives you all this information and more. It covers the basic equipment required for stocking up your store cupboard, buying, storing and preparing fruit and vegetables, and general advice on food juices.

Juice Up Your Energy Levels is simple, attainable and achievable. It's not a prescription for dreary, tasteless juices that are a chore to prepare, but a stunning selection of fun, delicious food drinks that are a pleasure to indulge in!

CHAPTER ONE

Just for Starters

THE JUICE KITCHEN

This chapter looks at the kitchen equipment essentials for food juices. It also provides a guide to what to keep in your larder, how to buy and store fruit, vegetables, herbs and spices, and buying fresh juices as a base for some instant food juices.

KITCHEN UTENSILS FOR FOOD JUICES

To equip your juice kitchen all you need is a handful of utensils. The expensive juicer is not required for the majority of these food juices. (If you are interested in investing in a juicer, see Chapter Eight for more information).

You may already have many of these items. If not, they will make a really useful addition to your kitchen, not only for food juices, but also for everyday cooking.

Liquidiser or Food Processor
If I had the choice between one of these, I would certainly choose a liquidiser, as it gives a finer food juice. A food processor, however, will still give an excellent result, just a slightly coarser texture.

Sharp Knife

It is worth investing in at least one small sharp knife. A lot of fruit, and especially vegetables, have fairly tough skins and a sharp knife really makes a difference. Slicing through a vegetable or chopping a fruit becomes a speedy, easy process and therefore hassle free.

Chopping Board

Wooden, plastic, coloured – it doesn't matter. Just make sure it's only used for raw fruit and vegetables. One word of advice: to stop your chopping board from sliding across your work top, place a damp cloth under it.

Small Scrubbing Brush for Vegetables

Many fruits and vegetables can be left with their skins on but they will require a good wash, and in some cases, a scrub.

Peeler

A lot of the goodness in fruit and vegetables is to be found just under the skin, so if you need to peel, be as light handed as possible. Many fruits can be placed in your blender unpeeled, but for those that do require peeling a good sharp peeler is essential.

Sieve

When buying a sieve, choose one that's stainless steel and strong. Its major use for these food juices is, of course, straining, but it can also double up as a colander for washing fruit and vegetables.

Spoons, Spatulas and Whisks
All these utensils are best in wood or plastic, and kept just for food juicing purposes.

Measuring Jug
A jug with big, clear liquid measurements not only makes for accurate measuring, but also serves as a container for the finished juice.

Grater
A stainless steel, free-standing grater is best. Use a pastry brush to remove the citrus zest from your grater – this enables you to get the maximum amount of zest and helps with the washing up too!

Lemon Juicer
Finally, a lemon juicer is a good tool or, if you're feeling strong, use your hands!

JUICY ADVICE

Five reasons why fruits and vegetables will juice up your energy levels. They are:
- A great provider of dietary fibre
- Rich in minerals and vitamins
- A pleasure to touch and smell
- A great way to keep the body well watered
- Low in fat

DRINKING YOUR JUICES

Turn Off the Tap
- When addding water to your food juices always use still or sparkling mineral water.
- Each recipe will give you a guide to adding water. The amount of water can be altered to your taste for a more or less concentrated flavour.

To Strain or Not to Strain
Juices do not always have to be strained. Leave unstrained if a more textured consistency is required.

Serving
Juices must be served and drunk immediately and never left to stand, even in a fridge. If you like chilled juice, serve it in a chilled glass or over ice.

Digestion
To aid digestion, do not drink food juices with your main meals. They are always best drunk an hour or so before or after, 'solo style'.

Take pleasure in your juice. Don't gulp it down, sip it and allow the goodness to be digested.

BUYING AND STORING FRUIT AND VEGETABLES

Any good chef will tell you that the secret to a successful recipe lies first and foremost in the quality of the ingredients.

FRUIT BUYING

- Fruit should not be bruised or have a broken skin.
- Fruit should have a firm, juicy unwrinkled texture and be a good weight for its size.
- Some fruits such as melons and pineapple give off a sweet swell when ripe and ready for eating.
- Berries should be plump, but dry.

Fresh Facts
Here are some tips for buying and storing fresh fruit and vegetables.

FRUIT STORING

- Remove all plastic packaging to allow the fruit to breathe.
- Spring clean your fruit bowl regularly and keep out of direct sunlight.
- Store at room temperature if you wish your fruit to ripen.
- To delay your fruit ripening, refrigerate. The exceptions to this are avocados or bananas, which should never be refrigerated.

VEGETABLE BUYING

- Root vegetables should be firm and have no damage to the surface.
- Leaf and salad vegetables should be fresh and sprightly looking, never limp or shrivelled.
- Fruit and vegetables should have smooth, glossy skins.

VEGETABLE STORING

- Again, remove all plastic packaging to allow the vegetables to breathe.
- Root vegetables can be kept in a cool, dark place.
- Leaf salad is best kept in the refrigerator, and this also applies to cauliflower and broccoli.

> *Organic or Not?*
> **The answer to this question is yes, of course, organic is better... if you can find and afford it!**

THE RIGHT STUFF

FRUITS

Apples

The apple was first introduced to us by the Romans. The king of fruits is extremely versatile and can be used in many dishes, but more importantly makes great juice. Nutritionally apples are low in calories and contain vitamin C, so perhaps there is a great deal of truth in the saying, 'To eat an apple a day, going to bed, will make the doctor beg his bread.' For juicing, make sure apples are fresh and as recently purchased as possible. Choose apples that are undamaged and bruise free.

Apricots

To get the most from your apricots when juicing, choose ones with a rich orange hue that give slightly under the thumb – these are the ripest. Apricots do not keep for long, especially in a bowl of fruit, where they will overripen and wrinkle. To store for a couple of days, keep in a plastic bag in the fridge. Apricots have a high level of potassium and contain fibre.

Bananas

For juicing, choose bananas that have a deep yellow, slightly freckled skin. Bananas whose skins are more brown and black than yellow are overripe and can be bitter and rancid. Bananas are said to be good for the stomach and contain carbohydrate for energy.

Blackberries

Sweet and juicy, these plump delicious berries can not only be purchased, but grow wild in the late summer months. When buying or picking blackberries, choose ones which are black with no hint of red or green. Check for mould or maggots.

Blueberries

A good source of vitamin C, in some Scandinavian countries they are used as a natural remedy for diarrhoea! Whatever your reason, they make a great drink. These bloomy berries are hardier than most, and can be kept for several days in the fridge.

Sweet Cherries

When choosing your cherries, check that the stems are green, as these show the cherries are fairly fresh. Eat or juice your cherries within two days of purchase. This plump juicy fruit has a sweet-sour kick that marries well with other fruits for juicing.

Cranberries

This tart, hard berry is known as a natural treatment for urinary infections. It has a very strong flavour which can be overbearing, so use in moderation, or mix and match!

Grapes

Without a doubt, grapes are best consumed uncooked, and the way to choose them is to taste them! They should be sweet and juicy and will make an excellent partner for many other fruits and vegetables.

Grapefruit

Yellow ones can be very sharp, whilst the pink variety is sweeter, but both make very refreshing juice drinks. Grapefruits yield a good amount of juice – choose ones that are plump in appearance and heavy for their size.

Kiwi

The furry brown skin of these fruits encases a flesh rich in vitamin C. They are no longer considered an unusual fruit as they are now reasonably priced and available all year round.

Lemons and Limes

These sharp, citrus fruits add zing and zest to everyday juices, but take care – a little goes a long way. Try lemon juice in a glass of warm water, with a spoonful of runny honey as a refreshing winter warmer. Pick lemons and limes that have a thin skin and feel heavy for their size.

Mango

Ripe mangoes are not defined by their skin colour, but by the feel of the flesh: the skin should give slightly under the pressure of your thumb. Pick and choose carefully – they are not cheap – but the nectar you'll gain from juicing this fruit is worth every penny.

Melon

With a high water content and rich in vitamins B and C, this fruit comes in many shapes and forms. Test for ripeness as you would for mangoes. Juice enthusiasts claim that the bulk of the goodness lies on and just under the skin. However, to juice a whole melon, an electric juicer is essential. Melons have a strong smell and should be kept away from other fruits.

Nectarines

Similar to a peach in flavour but with a nutty hint, these juicy fruits produce great drinks. Choose ripe nectarines for the fullest flavour and make the most of them during the summer months when they are abundant and at their best.

Oranges

As well as making an excellent base juice, oranges are rich in vitamin C. The juice of the orange has a delicate citrus fruit flavour. Should you desire a more pungent flavour to your juice, wash and dry the orange well before grating off and adding the zest.

Passion Fruit

This small, brown fruit contains the most delicious pulp with edible pips. Cut in half and, using a teaspoon, scoop out the pulp and pips and transform your juices into something truly exotic. Choose fruits with a dimpled skin that are heavy for their size.

Papaya

Also known as paw paw. When choosing papaya, follow the same rules as for avocado. The flesh should give slightly under the thumb and the fruit should be juiced within a couple of days of purchase. Juice only the flesh and not the skin or the seeds.

Peach

Peaches are a scrumptious summer fruit that make a lucious rich drink. Choose fruits with perfect, unblemished skins and use as soon as they are ripe.

Pears

This old faithful fruit is available all year round. The delicate flavour of the pear makes it as versatile, and as useful, as the apple for juicing. Like apple juice it deteriorates very quickly, so once juiced, drink immediately.

Pineapple

As well as tasting refreshingly good, pineapples contain vitamin C and are also thought to help digestion. A pineapple, when ready to eat or juice, will have a sweet seductive smell and the leaves will be easy to remove from the crown.

Plums

The juiciest, sweetest plums will be plump and ripe, the skin giving slightly on pressure. If purchased like this then juice immediately. A good source of dietary fibre, unripe plums can be stored for up to a week until ripened and ready.

Raspberries

Never in season for long enough! Fortunately, raspberries are available frozen all year round and these work just as well in juice drinks. The seeds are edible, although they can be strained out if you like a smoother texture. However, by doing this you may reduce the fibre content.

Rhubarb

Rhubarb is not really a fruit but a vegetable. Rich in essential vitamins and minerals, rhubarb should not be considered suitable as a daily juice. Consume in moderation and never juice the leaves as they are very poisonous.

Strawberries

Available now in all shapes and sizes, choose the ripest, most succulent specimens for juicing. Normally considered a dessert fruit, strawberries have a peppery kick and make excellent salad dressing. (See Chapter Six)

VEGETABLES

Avocado
Delicious and savoury in flavour, avocados are officially a fruit. They are rich in the good mono-unsaturated fats that are also found in olive oil. Use when just soft. Overripe and bruised fruit has a rancid flavour.

Beansprouts
Great in salads and stirfries, beansprouts also lend an excellent peppery flavour to juice drinks. Always rinse well before use and only keep for a day or so after purchase.

Beetroot
This stunning purple root vegetable can be used in juice drinks raw or cooked – the former being better for you and more delicious. A rich source of vitamin C and minerals, beetroot juice has a reputation for purging the system, so beware – a little goes a long way.

Broccoli
Once purchased, use broccoli within a couple of days as it deteriorates quickly. There has been much written about broccoli's potential anti-cancer links. Whatever the claims, like many dark green vegetables it is a great source of vitamins A, B and C.

Carrot
If there's one organic vegetable you should always buy it's carrots, as they are reasonably priced and readily available. If your carrots aren't organic, be sure to peel them before juicing. Rich in vitamins A and C, carrot juice makes a delicious starter juice on its own or combined with other flavours.

Celery

When buying celery, the key word is crisp. Soft and bendy will not do! Don't forget to include the leafy tops in your juice.

Cucumber

If your cucumber is not organic, be sure to peel it. This vegetable has a high water content and contains vitamins C and mineral salts. Use as a skin toner as well as a refreshing juice and treat the body outside and in.

Fennel

Some say that fennel is a great treatment for heartburn. Its unique, sweet, aniseed flavour can be used to liven up less flavoursome juices.

Garlic

Garlic is said to have many health-giving properties, from being a natural antiseptic to thinning the blood. Remember to rinse your blender or juicer immediately after use, as garlic has a strong flavour which will dominate others.

Lettuce

You can use many varieties of lettuce for juicing. Ensure the leaves are crisp and fresh and free from damage. Use the outer leaves if possible as they contain more goodness.

Onions

Know your onions: strong, mild, red or spring! Don't just keep them for cooking – they pep up many savoury juices, and have a great medical history.

Parsnip

Yes, parsnips! Raw parsnips can be juiced to make a surprisingly delicious drink. Use small parsnips for the sweetest juice and test out the claim that they strengthen your hair and nails.

Peppers

Sweet peppers are as good a source of vitamin C as oranges. With the exception of the green pepper, their juice is sweet and is excellent blended with other salad ingredients.

Radish

Hot and fiery, radishes make a peppery juice drink. Choose small ones – as a rule the larger radishes have less flavour.

Spinach

Choose baby leaves and combine with other vegetables. Spinach contains vitamins A and C, but drink in moderation – it has a dramatic effect on your system!

Sweet Potato

Another vegetable you would perhaps never have thought of juicing. Once a rarity, sweet potato is now widely available. The juice is sweet and combines well with fruits and ginger.

Tomato

An excellent source of vitamins A and C, for good juice you need ripe tomatoes with taste. There are now many flavoursome varieties of tomato to choose from. To ripen green tomatoes, simply place them on a sunny windowsill.

Watercress

Having a slightly bitter taste, watercress is best married with sweeter companions, such as pears, red or green apples or carrots. Use within two days of purchase and keep in the fridge until required.

FRUIT AND VEGETABLE PREPARATION

- For best results remove all fruit and vegetables from the fridge and bring to room temperature before juicing.
- All fruit and salad should be washed well to remove any surface residue.
- Vegetables should be given a wash and a good scrub.
- Wash and scrub your fruit and vegetables under cold running water. Do not allow them to soak.
- Fruit and vegetables with inedible or hard skins should be peeled before juicing. Each recipe will give you a guideline for the fruits it includes.

THE JUICE LARDER

A larder may sound like a thing from the past, but a well-stocked larder, in your cupboard, fridge and freezer, is a great back-up for the inventive juicer. Listed below are some important tips for building the foundations of an abundant larder which will enable you to be more creative, organised and impromptu in your juice kitchen.

- Utilise your cupboard space effectively by spring cleaning regularly.
- Clear out any old unused equipment.
- Throw away goods past their sell-by dates.

- Make your new-found space user-friendly, allowing quick stock checks and easy access. Flavourings and spices should both have their own space.

Buying Fresh Juices

Store cupboard long-life juices are a great back-up. However, when buying back-up juices it's best to choose either freshly squeezed or those with a longer life but not made from concentrate.

Frozen Fruits

Whether picked fresh from the garden or bought from the supermarket, frozen fruits make excellent bases for exciting cocktails and smoothies. My favourite frozen standbys are an exotic fruit mix and simple raspberries.

Canned Fruits

Apricots, blackcurrants, blackberries, peaches to name but a few. But make sure you use canned fruits in natural juice and not sugar syrup.

Herbs and Dried Spices

Spices

These aromatic seasonings should be bought in small quantities, especially if ground. Always store in an airtight glass jar well away from heat and light. Do not keep for more than six months.

Herbs

Herbs should always be fresh. If you have some herbs growing in your garden in the summer, or buy more than you need, don't forget to freeze any excess so you have a year-round store.

CHAPTER TWO

Just for Kicks

A mixture of exciting concoctions, from Simply Spinach to the Great Grape, this chapter is a great introduction to the juice world, and from the very beginning demonstrates how quick and easy food juices really are. In no time at all you'll be hooked and quenching your thirst with canned fizz will be a thing of the past. Whizz your way through this chapter and put a spring back in your step.

FRUIT AND ONE VEG   *serves 1–2*

Everyday ingredients combine to create this simple but truly refreshing fruit and vegetable concoction. This is the ideal first juice to get you hooked!

INGREDIENTS
- 1 dessert apple, roughly chopped
- 1 orange, peeled and roughly chopped
- 1 carrot, peeled and grated
- 150ml (5floz) still mineral water

METHOD
Place all the ingredients in a liquidiser or blender and whizz for 30 seconds. Strain through a sieve and serve immediately.

VERY SAVOURY   *serves 1–2*

Fennel is said to help digestion. It is best eaten raw and gives an aniseed twang to this vegetable juice. If you're taken with the taste, try it thinly sliced and tossed with your favourite salad ingredients.

INGREDIENTS
- 1/2 bulb fennel, trimmed and roughly chopped
- 2 large ripe tomatoes, roughly chopped
- 1 carrot, peeled and grated
- 125ml (4floz) still mineral water

METHOD
Place all the ingredients in a liquidiser or blender and whizz for 30 seconds. Strain through a sieve and serve immediately.

GREAT GRAPE

serves 1–2

Citrus and sweet with a herby kick, the pith of the grapefruit adds texture and goodness to this juice – don't be tempted to remove it! The grapes give a subtle sweetness to the grapefruit hit.

INGREDIENTS

- 110g (4oz) white seedless grapes
- 1/2 grapefruit, peeled and roughly chopped
- 1 tablespoon mint leaves
- 80ml (3floz) still mineral water

METHOD

Place all the ingredients in a liquidiser or blender and whizz for 30 seconds. Strain through a sieve and serve immediately.

THE CITRUS HIT

serves 1–2

Freshly squeezed orange juice is the traditional vitamin C drink. For an extra hit, add a kick of refreshing lime. If you fancy a little fizz, replace the still mineral water with the sparkling variety.

INGREDIENTS
- 3 oranges, peeled and roughly chopped
- juice 1 lime
- 80ml (3floz) still mineral water

METHOD
Place all the ingredients in a liquidiser or blender and whizz for 30 seconds. Strain through a sieve and serve immediately.

TOMATO STINGER

serves 1–2

Luscious, ripe tomatoes make a rich, satisfying drink. Ensure you buy a flavoursome variety or leave them on your kitchen windowsill to catch the sun and ripen. The amount of tabasco sauce gives a fairly mild sting – add more if you're feeling brave!

INGREDIENTS
- 3 large, ripe tomatoes, roughly chopped
- 1 tablespoon basil leaves
- a dash of tabasco sauce, or mild chilli sauce
- 80ml (3floz) still mineral water

METHOD
Place all the ingredients in a liquidiser or blender and whizz for 30 seconds. Strain through a sieve and serve immediately.

SIMPLY SPINACH

serves 1–2

Don't cook these dark green leaves, juice them! Spinach is best eaten raw to allow your body to gain maximum benefit from all its natural goodness.

INGREDIENTS
- A generous handful baby spinach leaves
- 2 oranges, peeled and roughly chopped
- 1 small dessert apple, roughly chopped
- 125ml (4floz) still mineral water

METHOD
Place all the ingredients in a liquidiser or blender and whizz for 30 seconds. Strain through a sieve and serve immediately.

THE CRUNCH

serves 1–2

For maximum taste don't discard the celery leaves, which have a delicious flavour. You can combine celery with carrot instead of apple to give an added sweetness to this juice.

INGREDIENTS
- 2 large sticks celery with leaves, roughly chopped
- 1 dessert apple, roughly chopped
- 150ml (5floz) still mineral water

METHOD
Place all the ingredients in a liquidiser or blender and whizz for 30 seconds. Strain through a sieve and serve immediately.

THINK PINK

serves 1–2

Grapefruit juice is not just for the start of the day. Sweeter than the classic paler variety, pink grapefruit has an attractive colour and makes a juice that's gentler on the taste buds.

INGREDIENTS

- 1 pink grapefruit, peeled and roughly chopped
- 1 dessert apple, roughly chopped
- 80ml (3floz) still mineral water

METHOD

Place all the ingredients in a liquidiser or blender and whizz for 30 seconds. Strain through a sieve and serve immediately.

GOING BANANAS

serves 1–2

Ripe bananas are a must for this luscious juice, as unripe, they are bland and lack that rich sweetness. Choose the ones with brown freckles on their skins. Bananas are high in carbohydrate and make a filling juice, perfect for when your stomach's really rumbling!

INGREDIENTS

- 1 ripe banana, peeled and roughly chopped
- 1 orange, peeled and roughly chopped
- juice 1/2 lime
- 80ml (3floz) still mineral water

METHOD

Place all the ingredients in a liquidiser or blender and whizz for 30 seconds. Strain through a sieve and serve immediately.

SALAD COOLER
serves 1–2

Round, Cos, Webb, Chinese, Iceberg – all these lettuces make great juice. The secret is to use the outer leaves, which have more of the goodness, so don't throw them away! The cucumber gives a coolness to this juice and the spring onion a gentle zing.

INGREDIENTS
- 6 large lettuce leaves
- 1/4 cucumber, roughly chopped
- 2 spring onions, roughly chopped
- 125ml (4floz) still mineral water

METHOD
Place all the ingredients in a liquidiser or blender and whizz for 30 seconds. Strain through a sieve and serve immediately.

NO MORE TEARS
serves 1–2

Onions have a great medical and kitchen history. Red onion and orange combined is one of my favourite salads. If you know and love your onions try this pungent, instant juice that won't bring tears to your eyes!

INGREDIENTS
- 1 red onion, peeled and roughly chopped
- 2 oranges, peeled and roughly chopped
- 150ml (5floz) still mineral water

METHOD
Place all the ingredients in a liquidiser or blender and whizz for 30 seconds. Strain through a sieve and serve immediately.

PASSION FOR PINEAPPLE *serves 2–3*

It is said that both pineapple and ginger act as digestive aids and they make a delicious combination. The top tip here is to choose a ripe pineapple, determined by the sweet, warm smell and the easy removal of a leaf from the crown.

INGREDIENTS
- 1 small ripe pineapple, peeled and chopped
- 2.5cm (1 inch) piece ginger, peeled and roughly chopped
- 175ml (6floz) still mineral water

METHOD
Place all the ingredients in a liquidiser or blender and whizz for 30 seconds. Strain through a sieve and serve immediately.

CHAPTER THREE

Souper Smoothies

A fusion of flavours from around the world – thick, rich, creamy and smooth, these souper smoothies are much more than a drink. Serve these bowls of goodness as a starter, snack, supper or pudding, or whenever takes your fancy.

RED DEVIL SMOOTHIE   *serves* 2

••

Based on the classic Russian dish, Bortsch, this smoothie can
be gently heated and served warm, before adding the yoghurt
and dill.

INGREDIENTS
- 110g (4oz) cooked beetroot, roughly chopped
- 1 tablespoon fresh dill tips
- 125ml (4floz) still mineral water
- 1/4 cucumber, roughly chopped
- 2 tablespoons natural yoghurt
- extra fresh dill tips, for garnish
- salt and freshly ground black pepper

METHOD
In a liquidiser or blender, whizz the beetroot, dill, water and
cucumber until smooth. Season well.

Transfer the beetroot smoothie to two bowls and serve
topped with a dollop of the yoghurt and a generous scattering
of fresh dill tips.

MEXICAN SALSA SMOOTHIE *serves 2*

• •

This deliciously rich, Mexican-style smoothie will satisfy the largest of appetites. The success of this smoothie depends on the ripeness of the avocado pear. Gently press the avocado at the stem end to check it gives only slightly under your thumb.

INGREDIENTS

• 1 ripe avocado, peeled and diced
• 2 ripe tomatoes, diced
• 2 tablespoons fresh coriander
• juice 1/2 lime
• 60ml (2floz) tomato juice
• tabasco sauce to taste
• salt and freshly ground black pepper
• olive oil to garnish

METHOD

In a bowl, combine a small amount of the prepared avocado, tomato and coriander and reserve for the garnish. In a liquidiser or blender, whizz together the remaining avocado, tomato, coriander, lime juice, tomato juice and tabasco sauce until smooth. Season.

Transfer the avocado smoothie to two serving bowls and top with the reserved garnish. Drizzle over a little olive oil, grind over some black pepper and serve at once.

GREEK GODDESS SMOOTHIE *serves* 2

This Greek-style smoothie is based on the traditional dish Tzatziki. The addition of watercress gives it a clean, refreshing and slightly peppery flavour.

INGREDIENTS
- 2 tablespoons finely diced cucumber
- 3 tablespoons Greek yoghurt or bio yoghurt
- 55g (2oz) watercress
- 175ml (6floz) fresh orange juice
- salt and freshly ground black pepper

METHOD
In a bowl, combine the cucumber with two tablespoons of the yoghurt. Set to one side. In a liquidiser or blender whizz together the remaining yoghurt, watercress and orange juice. Season well.

Serve the smoothie in bowls topped with the Greek yoghurt and cucumber.

GINGERED APPLE CHUNKY *serves* 4

••

Perhaps this recipe should not be in the smoothie chapter.
It can be whizzed smooth if you like, but I prefer it with a
chunky texture.

INGREDIENTS

- 2 dessert apples, cored and roughly chopped
- 2 large sticks celery with leaves, roughly chopped with
  the leaves reserved for garnish
- 2 ripe tomatoes, roughly chopped
- 1 clove garlic, peeled and roughly chopped
- 2.5cm (1 inch) ginger, peeled and roughly chopped
- 1 red chilli, halved, de-seeded and roughly chopped
- 175ml (6floz) apple juice
- Salt and freshly ground black pepper

METHOD

Place all the ingredients in a liquidiser or blender. Whizz briefly
until just combined, but still slighly chunky. Season.
    Serve garnished with the reserved celery leaves.

ORANGE AND ALMOND NECTAR

serves 2

Luscious and thick, this nutty nectar has added protein in the form of almonds.

INGREDIENTS

- 30g (1oz) flaked almonds, toasted
- 2 ripe nectarines, stoned and roughly chopped
- 1 orange, peeled and roughly chopped
- 60ml (2 floz) still mineral water
- squeeze lemon juice

METHOD

In a liquidiser or blender place half the toasted almonds, the nectarines, orange, mineral water and lemon juice. Whizz until smooth.

Transfer the nectar to serving bowls and scatter over the remaining almonds.

PLUMMY PEAR SMOOTHIE *serves* 2

∙∙

Ripe and succulent fruits, finished with a flourish of shelled pistachios.

INGREDIENTS
- 1 ripe dessert pear, cored and roughly chopped
- 2 ripe plums, stoned and roughly chopped
- 80ml (3floz) fresh orange juice
- $1/2$ oz pistachios, shelled and roughly chopped

METHOD
In a liquidiser or blender, place the pear, plums and orange juice. Whizz until smooth.

Transfer the pear and plum smoothie to serving bowls and scatter over the pistachios.

ORIENTAL SMOOTHIE   *serves* 4

A smoothie with a hint of the orient. No chopsticks required!

INGREDIENTS
- 175g (6oz) beansprouts
- 175g (6oz) snowpeas
- 1 clove garlic, peeled and roughly chopped
- juice 1 orange
- 215 ml (7floz) still mineral water
- $1/2$ teaspoon sesame oil
- 30g (1oz) sesame seeds, toasted
- salt and freshly ground black pepper

METHOD
In a liquidiser or blender, place the beansprouts, snow peas, garlic, orange juice and water. Whizz until smooth.

Transfer the oriental smoothie to four Chinese bowls or large teacups, drizzle over the sesame oil and sprinkle with the warm sesame seeds.

A TASTE OF THE TROPICS *serves* 2

A smooth, velvety concoction with a tropical taste.

INGREDIENTS
- 1 ripe banana, peeled and roughly chopped
- 1 ripe medium mango, peeled with the flesh sliced away from stone
- grated zest and juice $1/2$ lime
- 60ml (2floz) orange juice
- extra lime zest for garnish

METHOD
In a liquidiser or blender, place the banana, mango, lime juice, zest and orange juice. Whizz until smooth.

Serve the banana and mango smoothie in soup bowls and garnish with the extra lime zest.

A NICE PEAR   *serves* 2

Avocados are classed as a fruit and not a vegetable. They are rich in oils and deliciously versatile in a range of dishes, such as dips, salads, or even grilled with cheese.

This recipe is one of my favourites – simply serve in a bowl with a spoon.

INGREDIENTS

- 1 orange pepper, cored and deseeded
- 1 ripe avocado, peeled with stone removed
- 1 teaspoon coriander seeds
- juice 1/2 lemon
- 60ml (2floz) still mineral water
- salt and freshly ground black pepper
- grated lemon rind and black pepper to garnish

METHOD

In a liquidiser or blender, place the orange pepper, avocado, coriander seeds, lemon juice and water and whizz until smooth. Season well.

Transfer to soup bowls, sprinkle on the grated lemon rind and grind over some black pepper.

FRUIT FOOL

serves 2

Truly more of a juicy pudding than a smoothie. For special occasions serve in tall chilled glasses with your favourite biscuits for dipping.

INGREDIENTS

- 55g (2oz) sultanas
- 2 ripe bananas, peeled and roughly chopped
- 3 tablespoons fromage frais
- 125ml (4floz) freshly squeezed orange juice

METHOD

Place half of the sultanas in a bowl and pour over the orange juice. Set to one side for 15 minutes.

In a liquidiser or blender place the bananas and half the fromage frais. Add the soaked sultanas and orange juice and whizz until smooth.

Serve the banana and sultana fool in chilled glasses, spoon a dollop of fromage frais into each glass and sprinkle on the remaining sultanas.

BLACK FOREST SOUP *serves* 2

Cherries and berries combine in this vibrant, stunning
smoothie. Tart and refreshing – you have to have a really
sweet tooth to finish with a drizzling of runny honey.

INGREDIENTS

- 55g (2oz) cherries, pitted
- 55g (2oz) strawberries
- 55g (2oz) raspberries
- 55g (2oz) blueberries
- 60ml (2floz) white grape juice
- 1 tablespoon crème fraîche

METHOD

Reserve a small amount of the berries for the garnish and
place the remaining cherries, strawberries, raspberries, blueberries and grape juice in a liquidiser or blender. Whizz until
smooth. This smoothie contains pips, so if a smooth texture is
required, strain through a sieve.

Transfer the Black Forest soup to dessert bowls. Top each
bowl with a spoonful of crème fraîche and scatter over the
reserved berries.

STRAWBERRIES WITHOUT THE CREAM

serves 2

A light grinding of fresh black pepper over your strawberries, in place of clotted cream, is surprisingly good.

INGREDIENTS
- 225g (8oz) strawberries, hulled
- 2 large kiwis, peeled and chopped
- juice of 2 oranges
- 150ml (5floz) still mineral water
- freshly ground black pepper

METHOD
Place the strawberries, kiwis, orange juice and water in a liquidiser or blender. Whizz until smooth.

Pour into soup bowls and finish with a grinding of freshly ground black pepper.

BLUEBERRY PIE

A delicious blueberry pudding.

INGREDIENTS

- 225g (8oz) blueberries
- 2 small ripe bananas, peeled
- 300ml ($1/2$ pint) orange juice
- 2 scoops of vanilla ice-cream

METHOD

Reserve a handful of blueberries for the garnish and place the remaining blueberries, bananas and orange juice in a liquidiser or blender and whizz until smooth.

Transfer the smoothie to two dessert bowls and sprinkle with the reserved blueberries. Float a scoop of vanilla ice-cream on the top and serve at once.

CHAPTER FOUR

Fruit Cocktails

Threw cocktail hour has arrived! Shaken, stirred or whizzed, these stylish cocktails can be rounded off with a shot of spirit if so desired. Serve in chilled, decorated glasses accompanied by a canapé or two. Chin-chin!

TROPICAL FRUIT CUP   *serves* 2

Tantalising tropical fizz.

INGREDIENTS
- 175g (6oz) tropical frozen fruits, slightly thawed
- 2–3 teaspoons runny honey
- 500ml (16floz) sparkling mineral water
- lime slices to garnish

METHOD
In a liquidiser or blender, place the tropical fruits, runny honey and 6 tablespoons of the mineral water. Whizz briefly until just smooth.

Pour the tropical fruit base into two cocktail glasses, top up with sparkling mineral water to taste, and garnish each glass with a slice of lime.

RASPBERRY FRUIT CUP   *serves* 2

INGREDIENTS
- 110g (4oz) frozen raspberries, slightly thawed
- 2–3 tablespoons maple syrup
- 500ml (16floz) sparkling mineral water
- a few thawed, whole raspberries and fresh mint leaves
  to garnish

METHOD
Place the raspberries, maple syrup and 4 tablespoons of
the mineral water in a liquidiser or blender. Blend briefly
until just smooth. If you require a smoother cocktail, add a
little more water to the liquidiser or blender and then strain
through a sieve.

Pour the raspberry base into two cocktail glasses, top up
with sparkling mineral water to taste, and garnish with the
whole raspberries and fresh mint leaves.

SPICY MARY

serves 2

A hot and spicy version of the alcoholic cocktail, served on crushed ice.

INGREDIENTS

- 300ml (10floz) tomato juice
- 2 large tomatoes, roughly chopped
- juice 1 lime
- 1 red chilli, deseeded and roughly chopped
- 1 teaspoon sugar

METHOD

In a liquidiser or blender, place the tomato juice, tomatoes, lime juice, chilli and sugar. Whizz until smooth.

Half fill two cocktail glasses with crushed ice. Pour the Spicy Mary over the crushed ice and serve at once.

CRANBERRY SOUR

serves 2

This sweet and sour cocktail will put a spring in your step!
Not for those with a very sweet tooth.

INGREDIENTS
- 175g (6oz) frozen cranberries, slightly thawed
- juice 2 limes
- 2 teaspoons honey
- 250ml (8floz) soda water
- 1 tablespoon salt
- sliced strawberries or blueberries to garnish

METHOD
In the liquidiser or blender, place the cranberries, honey,
half the soda water and half the lime juice. Whizz together
until blended.

Meanwhile dip the rims of two glasses into the remaining
lime juice and then immediately into the salt, to create a salt-
rimmed glass. If this is too sour for you, you could use caster
sugar instead of the salt.

To serve, strain the cranberry fizz through a sieve into each
glass and top up with the remaining soda water. Serve at once.

CHERRY BERRY NECTAR   *serves* 2

A luxury fruit and nut nectar.

INGREDIENTS
- 175g (6oz) cherries, pitted
- 55g (2oz) strawberries
- 175ml (6floz) still mineral water
- 30g (1oz) flaked almonds, toasted

METHOD
Place the cherries, strawberries, mineral water and half the almonds in a liquidiser or blender. Whizz until smooth.

To serve, fill two glasses with crushed ice. Strain the cherry nectar over the crushed ice and sprinkle with the remaining flaked almonds.

LONG ISLAND KIWI AND CANTALOUPE

serves 2

A long, stylish cocktail to quench any thirst.

INGREDIENTS
- 285g (10oz) cantaloupe melon, peeled and roughly chopped
- 2 kiwi fruits, peeled and roughly chopped
- 300ml (10floz) orange juice
- orange slices to garnish

METHOD
In a liquidiser or blender, place the melon, kiwi fruit and orange juice. Whizz together until blended. This cocktail can be strained through a sieve if a smoother drink is required.

To serve, pour into long glasses and top up with a slice of orange.

CUCUMBER MINT COOLER *serves* 2

A cooling cocktail of apples, mint and cucumber.

INGREDIENTS
- 1/4 cucumber
- 300ml (10floz) clear apple juice
- 2 tablespoons mint leaves
- 1 small dessert apple, sliced

METHOD
Cut a few slices from the cucumber and set aside for the garnish. Roughly chop the remaining cucumber.

Place the roughly chopped cucumber, apple juice and mint leaves in a liquidiser or blender. Whizz until smooth.

Half fill two serving glasses with ice. Strain over the cocktail and garnish with the cucumber and apple slices.

PINK PANTHER

A luscious sweet foam. Very refreshing!

INGREDIENTS
- 85g (3oz) strawberries
- 110g (4oz) black seedless grapes
- 150ml (1/4 pint) still mineral water
- mint sprigs to garnish

METHOD
Place the strawberries, grapes and water in a liquidiser or blender. Whizz until smooth. This cocktail can be strained if a smoother drink is required.

Fill two glasses with crushed ice and pour over the cocktail. Garnish with the sprigs of mint.

PLUM GOOD

serves 2

An autumnal cocktail with a dash of spice!

INGREDIENTS
- 2 dessert apples, roughly chopped
- 4 ripe plums, stoned
- approx. 150ml (1/4 pint) sparkling mineral water
- shake of ground cinnamon

METHOD
Place the apples, plums and water in a liquidiser or blender. Whizz until smooth.

Fill two glasses with crushed ice and strain over the plum cocktail. Finish with a shake of ground cinnamon.

PASSION FRAPPÉ

serves 2

For those with a passion for mangoes!

INGREDIENTS
- 1 large ripe mango, peeled and cut away from the stone
- 2 passion fruit, flesh and pips scooped out
- 150ml (1/4 pint) still mineral water

METHOD
Place the mango, passion fruit and mineral water in a liquidiser or blender. Whizz until smooth.

Fill two cocktail glasses with crushed ice and pour over the mango frappé.

ICE BELLINI

serves 2

A yummy glass of peaches and cream.

INGREDIENTS
- 1 small ripe banana, peeled
- 1 small ripe peach, cut away from the stone
- 150ml (1/4 pint) orange juice
- 1–2 scoops frozen vanilla yoghurt

METHOD
Place the banana, peach and orange juice in a liquidiser or blender. Whizz until smooth. Add the frozen yoghurt and briefly whizz again.

Serve the Peach Bellini immediately over crushed ice.

FOREST FRUIT COLADA *serves 2*

Creamy fruits of the forest!

INGREDIENTS

- 180g (6oz) mixed fruits (blackberries, raspberries, redcurrants)
- 1 teaspoon runny honey
- 150ml (1/4 pint) orange juice
- 1–2 scoops frozen vanilla yoghurt

METHOD

Place the mixed fruits, honey, orange juice and frozen yoghurt in a liquidiser or blender. Whizz until smooth.

Fill two glasses with crushed ice and strain over the forest fruit colada.

APRICOT VELVET *serves 2*

A smooth orange liquor with a tangy kick.

INGREDIENTS
- 4 ripe apricots, stoned and quartered
- 1 dessert apple, roughly chopped
- 2 tangerines, peeled and segmented
- 150ml (1/4 pint) still mineral water

METHOD
Place the apricots, apple, tangerines and water in a liquidiser or blender. Whizz until smooth.

Strain the cocktail into glasses filled with crushed ice, and serve at once.

CHAPTER FIVE

Punch Drunk

I t's party time and these lively punches are refreshingly good. From the exotic Pineapple Pond or invigorating Grapefruit Lemonade to the warming Juniper Toddy, their taste and presentation make them suitable to grace any table at any gathering.

PINEAPPLE POND PUNCH *serves* 4

A tropical pool of luxury fruits.

INGREDIENTS
- 570ml (1 pint) orange juice
- 1 pineapple, peeled, cored and chopped
- 1 galia melon, deseeded, peeled and chopped
- 5cm (2 inches) fresh ginger, peeled and roughly chopped
- 2 handfuls fresh mint leaves

METHOD
In a large blender or food processor, place the orange juice, half the pineapple, half the melon, the fresh ginger and a handful of mint. Whizz together until blended and smooth.

If a smoother punch is required, strain through a sieve before pouring into a punch bowl or large serving bowl. Add the remaining chopped fruit and mint leaves to the punch and serve at once.

WATERMELON PUNCH POT *serves* 4–6

Served in its shell, this simple summer juice makes a stunning punch. Ladle into tall glasses or drink direct from the watermelon shell through long thick straws.

INGREDIENTS
- 1 watermelon
- juice 2 limes
- 6 strawberries

METHOD
Using a sharp knife, carefully slice a 'lid' from the top of the watermelon. Using a spoon, scoop out all the pink flesh from inside the melon, discarding the pips, and place in a large blender or food processor.

Add the lime juice to the blender and whizz with the watermelon flesh for 30 seconds.

To serve, pour the punch back into the watermelon shell. Float the strawberries on top and serve at once.

PASSION PUNCH   *serves 4–6*

Caribbean magic in the form of mangoes, bananas
and coconut.

INGREDIENTS
- 4 small ripe bananas, peeled and roughly chopped
- 2 ripe mangoes, peeled with the flesh cut away
  from the stone
- 300ml (10floz) coconut milk
- 300ml (10floz) orange juice
- 4 passion fruit flesh and pips, scooped out

METHOD
Place your serving glasses in the freezer for 20 minutes or
until well chilled.

In a large blender or food processor, place the bananas,
mango, coconut milk and orange juice. Whizz together
until smooth.

Pour the punch into a large punch bowl or serving bowl
and stir in the seeds and flesh of the passion fruit. Serve at
once in the frozen glasses.

MULLED FRUIT PUNCH *serves* 4

A perfect punch for chilly autumnal evenings.

INGREDIENTS

- 425ml (15floz) cranberry juice
- 150ml (5floz) orange juice
- 150ml (5floz) cloudy apple juice
- 1 orange
- 1 tablespoon cloves
- 1 large cinnamon stick

METHOD

Cut the orange in half and stud one half with the cloves. Cut the remaining orange into slices and place the orange half studded with cloves and the slices in a saucepan, along with the cinnamon stick.

Pour the cranberry, orange and apple juices over the fruit and spices and place the pan over a low heat. Heat the mulled punch until just boiling, then remove from the heat and leave to stand for ten minutes to allow the flavours to infuse.

Serve the warm mulled punch in heatproof glasses or cups, ensuring each serving has some sliced fruit.

JUNIPER TODDY

• •

Juniper berries give this hot toddy a gin flavour without
the alcohol. Even better with a wedge of warm shortbread
for dunking!

INGREDIENTS
- 425ml (15floz) orange juice
- 425ml (15floz) cloudy apple juice
- 8 juniper berries, crushed
- 1 large bay leaf
- 1 large sprig rosemary
- 1 ripe pear, cored and sliced

METHOD
In a large saucepan, place the orange and apple juices, juniper
berries, bay leaf and sprig of rosemary. Place the pan over a
low heat and heat gently until just boiling.

Remove the pan from the heat and set to one side for ten
minutes to allow the flavours to infuse. Serve the warm toddy
in teacups and saucers with a dessertspoon on the side.

GRAPEFRUIT LEMONADE *serves 4*

A sparkling, citrus lemonade for long hot summer days.

INGREDIENTS
- 2 fresh grapefruits
- 300ml (10floz) grapefruit juice
- 1 lemon, peeled and roughly chopped
- 2–3 tablespoons runny honey
- 150ml (5floz) sparkling mineral water

METHOD
Cut one of the grapefruits into thin slices. Set to one side. Peel the remaining grapefruit and roughly chop the flesh.

Place the grapefruit flesh, grapefruit juice, lemon and honey in a large blender or food processor. Whizz until smooth.

Strain the grapefruit lemonade through a sieve into a large punch or serving bowl. Top up with the sparkling mineral water and add the slices of grapefruit.

HI-THAI PUNCH

serves 4

A speedy Thai-style spritzer, whizzed up in seconds.

INGREDIENTS
- 300ml (10floz) orange juice
- 1/2 fresh pineapple, peeled and roughly chopped
- 1 ripe mango, peeled with the flesh cut away from the stone
- 2.5cm (1 inch) ginger, peeled and roughly chopped
- grated zest 1 lime
- 2 tablespoons fresh coriander leaves
- 150ml (1/4 pint) sparkling mineral water

METHOD
Place the all the ingredients in a large blender or food processor and whizz until blended together.

Serve this long cool punch in chilled glasses or over ice.

GOING BANANAS *serves 2–4*

A long milkshake-style punch! For a richer flavour, whizz in some vanilla ice-cream.

INGREDIENTS

- 425ml (15floz) orange juice
- 3 small ripe bananas, peeled
- 2 ripe peaches, stoned and roughly chopped
- fresh nutmeg for grating (optional)

METHOD

Place the orange juice, bananas and peaches in a large blender or food processor. Whizz until smooth.

Serve in long, tall glasses and grate over a touch of fresh nutmeg.

CHAPTER SIX

Juicy Dressings

J uices are not only for the glass. They make a great base for delicious dressings that can accompany an array of dishes: from the more usual salad, to grilled fish and meats, a sauce for baked potatoes and pasta, even a tasty dip. So get dressed for dinner!

OPEN SESAME! *serves* 4

The use of sesame oil and coriander lends this dressing an oriental flavour. Good served with grilled fish or chicken, this also makes a great salad dressing for Chinese lettuce and beansprouts.

INGREDIENTS
- 60ml (2floz) orange juice or the juice of 1 large orange
- 1 teaspoon sesame oil
- 2 tablespoons sunflower or olive oil
- handful fresh coriander leaves
- salt and freshly ground black pepper

METHOD
Place all the ingredients together in a liquidiser or blender. Whizz until smooth and season well.

STRAWBERRY BLUSH   *serves* 4

Strawberries make an interesting, peppery addition to this delicious, fruity pink dressing! This dressing works particularly well with avocado as a first course. Or try it as a refreshing accompaniment to garlic sausage.

INGREDIENTS
- 60ml (2floz) apple juice
- 2 large strawberries, roughly chopped
- 2 tablespoons olive oil
- salt and freshly ground black pepper

METHOD
Place all the ingredients together in a liquidiser or blender. Whizz until smooth and season well.

MOROCCAN JUICE   *serves* 4

The spice of the cumin and the sweetness of the carrot
give this dressing its Moroccan edge. Superb served with
chargrilled fish or chicken. Or double up the quantity and
stir through freshly cooked pasta.

INGREDIENTS
- 1 carrot, peeled and chopped
- 30ml (1floz) orange juice
- 2 tablespoons olive oil
- zest and juice 1 small lemon
- 1/2 teaspoon cumin
- salt and freshly ground black pepper

METHOD
Place all the ingredients together in a liquidiser or blender.
Whizz until smooth and season well.

CORIANDER AND GINGER PISTOU

serves 4

Serve this as a delicious accompaniment to panfried fish with new potatoes.

INGREDIENTS

- 2.5cm (1 inch) piece ginger, peeled and grated
- 1 tablespoon fresh coriander leaves
- juice 1 orange
- juice 1/2 lime
- 2 tablespoons sunflower oil
- salt and freshly ground black pepper

METHOD

Place all the ingredients together in a liquidiser or blender. Whizz until smooth and season well.

TOMATO PESTO

serves 4

A lighter style of pesto. Use as a delicious dressing for salad leaves or drizzle over a mozzarella, tomato and avocado salad.

INGREDIENTS

- 1 ripe plum tomato, roughly chopped
- 3 sprigs fresh basil
- juice 1/2 lemon
- 2 tablespoons olive oil
- pinch sugar
- salt and freshly ground black pepper

METHOD

Place all the ingredients together in a blender or liquidiser. Whizz until smooth and season well.

SOMERSET RELISH *serves* 4

Pep up your ploughman's lunch with this delicious salsa.
It goes particularly well with cheese of any type.

INGREDIENTS
- 80ml (3floz) apple juice
- 1 tablespoon olive oil
- splash cider vinegar
- 1/2 red apple, finely chopped
- 1 tablespoon toasted hazelnuts, chopped
- salt and freshly ground black pepper

METHOD
In a bowl, whisk together the apple juice, olive oil and cider vinegar.
Stir in the chopped apple and toasted hazelnuts and season well.

GREAT GRAPE SALSA *serves* 4

The dressing version of the Great Grape juice. Use it to replace
the bunch of grapes on your cheeseboard as it's particularly
good with any blue cheese.

INGREDIENTS
- 60ml (2floz) grapefruit juice
- 1 tablespoon fresh mint leaves
- 1 tablespoon olive oil
- 10 red and green seedless grapes, roughly chopped
- salt and freshly ground black pepper

METHOD
In a liquidiser or blender whizz together the grapefruit juice,
mint leaves and olive oil.
Stir in the grapes and season well.

PEAR AND POPPY SEED VINAIGRETTE

serves 4

The poppy seeds give this smooth pear vinaigrette a distinctive, nutty flavour.

INGREDIENTS

- 1 ripe pear, cored
- 60ml (2floz) apple juice
- juice 1 small lemon
- 1 tablespoon olive oil
- 1 tablespoon poppy seeds
- salt and freshly ground black pepper

METHOD

Finely chop half of the cored pear and set to one side.
Peel the remaining pear half and place it, roughly chopped, in a liquidiser or blender. Add the apple juice, lemon juice and olive oil and whizz together.

Transfer the dressing to a serving bowl, stir in the chopped pear and poppy seeds and season well.

PAPAYA AND WALNUT NECTAR

serves 4

An exotic fruity accompaniment makes a delicious dressing for a warm chicken or duck salad.

INGREDIENTS

- 80ml (3floz) orange juice
- 1/2 papaya, deseeded, peeled and roughly chopped
- 1 tablespoon olive oil
- 1/2 teaspoon walnut oil
- salt and freshly ground black pepper

METHOD

Place all the ingredients together in a liquidiser or blender. Whizz until smooth and season well.

GREEN WALNUT DRESSING _serves_ 4

A vibrant green sauce. Superb poured over freshly cooked new potatoes.

INGREDIENTS

- 40g (1 1/2oz) watercress, washed
- 30g (1oz) toasted walnuts
- 80ml (3floz) orange juice
- 1 tablespoon olive oil
- salt and freshly ground black pepper

METHOD

Place all the ingredients together in a liquidiser or blender. Whizz until smooth and season well.

AVOCADO MAYONNAISE   *serves* 4

The natural oils from the avocado give a richness to this
moreish mayonnaise.

INGREDIENTS
- 1 large ripe avocado, halved, stoned and peeled
- 80ml (3floz) orange juice
- 1 small ripe dessert pear, peeled, cored and chopped
- 1 tablespoon chopped chives
- salt and freshly ground black pepper

METHOD
Place all the ingredients together in a liquidiser or blender.
Whizz until smooth and season well.

MINT SAUCE   *serves* 4

A continental version of good old mint sauce. Particularly good
served with any Sunday roast.

INGREDIENTS
- 1 ripe plum tomato, chopped
- 1 small red onion, chopped
- 1/2 red pepper, roughly chopped
- 60ml (2floz) orange juice
- 3 tablespoons fresh mint leaves, chopped
- salt and freshly ground black pepper

METHOD
Place all the ingredients together in a liquidiser or blender.
Whizz until smooth and season well.

CHAPTER SEVEN

Flash Juices

This chapter uses carton juices as a base. Of course fresh is always best, but when time is of the essence, don't just reach for the canned fizz to quench your thirst – by adding something extra to these convenience juices you can whizz up delicious juice in no time!

FAST FRUIT CRUSH *serves 2*

The secret of this juice lies in the lemon and lime zest, so don't be tempted to leave it out!

INGREDIENTS
- 250ml (8floz) orange juice
- grated zest and juice 1 lemon
- grated zest and juice 1 lime

METHOD
Combine all the juices with the lemon and lime zest.
Serve at once over crushed ice.

APPLE JACK   *serves* 2

Apple is used in this thirst quencher to turn an everyday juice into something special.

INGREDIENTS
- 250ml (8floz) pink or ruby red grapefruit juice
- 1 dessert apple, cored and roughly chopped

METHOD
In a liquidiser or blender whizz the grapefruit juice with the apple. This juice will be slightly textured and can be sieved if a smooth texture is required. Serve at once.

LARDER JUICE   *serves* 2–3

A quick and easy luxury store-cupboard juice.

INGREDIENTS
- 250ml (8floz) orange juice
- 410g can apricots in natural juice, drained

METHOD
In a liquidiser or blender, whizz the orange juice with the apricots until smooth. Serve at once.

GINGER TOM

serves 2

The natural way to pep up your tommy juice.

INGREDIENTS
- 250ml (8floz) tomato juice
- 1.25cm (1/2 inch) piece ginger, peeled and roughly chopped

METHOD
In a liquidiser or blender, whizz the ginger into the tomato juice. Serve at once.

SWEET AND SOUR

serves 2

Fresh grapefruit gives a zingy lift to sweet pineapple.

INGREDIENTS
- 250ml (8floz) pineapple juice
- 1/2 grapefruit, peeled and roughly chopped

METHOD
Whizz the pineapple juice and grapefruit together in a liquidiser or blender. If a smoother texture is preferred, strain through a sieve. Serve at once.

CRANBERRY RELISH   *serves* 2

Classic cranberry and orange juice, enlivened with the addition of summer berries.

INGREDIENTS
- 250ml (8floz) cranberry juice
- 1 orange, peeled and roughly chopped
- 30g (1oz) strawberries or raspberries

METHOD
In a liquidiser or blender, place the cranberry juice, orange and strawberries or raspberries. Whizz until smooth. This juice may be sieved for a smoother texture. Serve at once.

PRICKLY PEAR   *serves* 2

The lime gives this subtle grape and pear juice its prickly edge.

INGREDIENTS
- 250ml (8floz) white grape juice
- 1 ripe dessert pear, cored and roughly chopped
- juice 1 lime

METHOD
In a liquidiser or blender, whizz the grape juice with the pear until smooth. Serve at once, adding a shot of lime juice to each glass to taste.

BUNNY JUICE   *serves* 2

Carrot and mandarins – a simple fruit and vegetable concoction.

INGREDIENTS
- 250ml (8floz) carrot juice
- 2 mandarin or tangerine oranges, peeled
  and roughly chopped

METHOD
In a liquidiser or blender, whizz together the carrot juice and
mandarin oranges. If you prefer a smoother texture, strain
through a sieve. Serve at once.

PALM CUP   *serves* 2

Transport yourself to the sun with this truly tropical juice.

INGREDIENTS
- 250ml (8floz) tropical fruit juice
- 80ml (3floz) coconut milk
- juice and grated zest 1 lime

METHOD
Place all the ingredients in a blender or liquidiser and whizz
together. Serve at once.

THE ITALIAN CONNECTION *serves* 2

Fresh basil gives this juice its Mediterranean flavour.

INGREDIENTS
- 250ml (8floz) orange juice
- 2 large tomatoes, roughly chopped
- handful fresh basil leaves

METHOD
Place the orange juice, tomatoes and basil leaves in a
liquidiser or blender. Whizz until smooth and serve at once.

GARDEN APPLE *serves* 2

A crisp, green, refreshing herbal juice.

INGREDIENTS
- 300ml (10floz) cloudy apple juice
- 1 dessertspoon fresh thyme leaves
- 1 dessertspoon fresh mint leaves

METHOD
In a liquidiser or blender, place the apple juice, thyme and
mint. Whizz together for 30 seconds until the herbs are
blended with the juice.

Pour into glasses and serve at once, while still frothy.

CHAPTER EIGHT

Nuts and Bolts

L ast, but certainly not least, the final chapter. The ultimate in juicing, the electric juicer, is without a doubt a must for food juice fans. Select your model carefully and choose the one that suits you best. Electric juicers come in all shapes and sizes and, of course, prices. They range from the simple citrus juicer to the serious, large centrifugal juicer for harder fruits and vegetables.

- For regular juicing a high-power motor is an important factor. A stronger motor will cope with most of the harder fruits and vegetables and will last longer. As with most of these kitchen gadgets, you get what you pay for.
- Pulp and juice-collecting containers can vary in size. A separate pulp collector is useful for juicing larger quantities and machines without this need dismantling before emptying.
- Remember, juicers must be cleaned between juicing and this means dismantling before cleaning. Check how your juicer dismantles. Is it easy and user-friendly?

- Check your instructions for cleaning. Many juicer parts cannot be put in the dishwasher and can make for a lot of washing-up. So make your life easy and clean your juicer immediately after use.
- When creating food juices the electric way remember the following points:
- You will find that juices in this chapter require slightly more fruit and vegetables and will therefore be stronger and more concentrated in flavour. Remember you can always add mineral water if you prefer a lighter result.
- The juices are more refined, and smoother in texture, than the juices you will have created so far.
- Juices should be drunk immediately and not stored.

SWEET POTATO, PEAR AND LIME
serves 2

INGREDIENTS
- 1 large sweet potato, cut into wedges
- 2 dessert pears, stalks removed and cut into wedges
- juice 1 lime

METHOD
Put the sweet potato and pears through the juicer.
Stir in the lime juice. Serve at once.

CELERY, CARROT AND APPLE

serves 2

INGREDIENTS
- 3 celery sticks with leaves, cut in half
- 2 carrots, cut into wedges
- 2 apples, stalks removed and cut into wedges

METHOD
Put the celery sticks, carrots and apples through the juicer.
Stir and serve at once.

BEETROOT, CARROT AND APPLE

serves 2

INGREDIENTS
- 2 raw beetroot, cut into wedges
- 4 carrots, cut into wedges
- 1 apple, stalk removed and cut into wedges

METHOD
Put the beetroot, carrots and apple through the juicer.
Stir and serve at once.

FENNEL AND RED PEPPER   *serves* 2

INGREDIENTS
- 1 small bulb fennel, cut into wedges
- 1 red pepper, stalk removed and cut into wedges
- 1 orange, peeled

METHOD
Put the fennel, red pepper and orange through the juicer.
Stir and serve at once.

CUCUMBER, WATERCRESS AND PEAR   *serves* 2

INGREDIENTS
- 3/4 cucumber, cut into wedges
- 1 pear, stalk removed and cut into wedges
- handful of watercress

METHOD
Put the cucumber, pear and watercress through the juicer.
Stir and serve at once.

SPINACH AND CARROT   *serves* 2

INGREDIENTS
- large handful of spinach leaves
- 4 carrots, cut into wedges
- 1 apple, stalk removed and cut into wedges

METHOD
Put the spinach, carrots and apple through the juicer.
Stir and serve at once.

LETTUCE, GREEN PEPPER AND APPLE   *serves* 2

INGREDIENTS
- 1 round lettuce, cut into wedges
- 1 green pepper, stalk removed and cut into wedges
- 1 dessert apple, stalk removed and cut into wedges

METHOD
Put the lettuce, pepper and apple through the juicer.
Stir and serve at once.

RADISH, APPLE
AND CARROT

serves 2

INGREDIENTS
- 1 bunch radishes, leaves removed
- 1 apple, stalk removed and cut into wedges
- 3 carrots, cut into wedges

METHOD
Put the radishes, apple and carrots through the juicer.
Stir and serve at once.

PARSNIP, CARROT
AND ORANGE

serves 2

INGREDIENTS
- 2 large parsnips, cut into wedges
- 1 carrot, cut into wedges
- 2 oranges, peeled

METHOD
Put the parsnips, carrot and oranges through the juicer.
Stir and serve at once.

APPLE, CARROT AND NUTMEG

serves 2

INGREDIENTS
- 2 apples, stalks removed and cut into wedges
- 3 carrots, cut into wedges
- grating of nutmeg

METHOD
Put the apples and carrots through the juicer.
Grate in the nutmeg, stir and serve at once.

BROCCOLI AND LETTUCE

serves 2

INGREDIENTS
- 175g (6oz) broccoli, roughly chopped
- 1/4 Iceberg lettuce, cut into wedges
- 1 apple, stalk removed and cut into wedges

METHOD
Put the broccoli, lettuce and apple through the juicer.
Stir and serve at once.

FENNEL, APPLE AND CUCUMBER

serves 2

INGREDIENTS

- 1 small bulb fennel, cut into wedges
- 1 apple, stalk removed and cut into wedges
- 1/2 cucumber, cut into wedges

METHOD

Put the fennel, apple and cucumber through the juicer.
Stir and serve at once.

RHUBARB, PEAR AND GINGER

serves 2

INGREDIENTS

- 2 stalks rhubarb, leaves removed
- 2 pears, stalks removed and cut into wedges
- 1 tablespoon chopped ginger

METHOD

Put the rhubarb, pears and ginger through the juicer.
Stir and serve at once.

APPLE, PLUM AND CINNAMON
serves 2

INGREDIENTS
- 3 apples, stalks removed and cut into wedges
- 4 plums, stoned
- 1 teaspoon cinnamon

METHOD
Put the apples and plums through the juicer.
Sprinkle over the cinnamon, stir and serve at once.

TOMATO AND CARROT
serves 2

INGREDIENTS
- 3 tomatoes, cut into wedges
- 3 carrots, cut into wedges

METHOD
Put the tomatoes and carrots through the juicer.
Stir and serve at once.

RED PEPPER, CARROT AND CELERY

serves 2

INGREDIENTS
- 1 red pepper, cut into wedges
- 2 carrots, cut into wedges
- 2 stalks celery, cut in half

METHOD
Put the pepper, carrots and celery through the juicer.
Stir and serve at once.

BEETROOT, APPLE AND CELERY

serves 2

INGREDIENTS
- 1 raw beetroot, cut into wedges
- 2 apples, cut into wedges
- 2 stalks celery

METHOD
Put the beetroot, apples and celery through the juicer.
Stir and serve at once.

BROCCOLI AND PEAR   *serves* 2

INGREDIENTS
- 175g (6oz) broccoli, roughly chopped
- 2 ripe pears, stalks removed and cut into wedges

METHOD
Put the broccoli and pears through the juicer.
Stir and serve at once.

PEAR, CARROT
AND PARSLEY   *serves* 2

INGREDIENTS
- 2 pears, stalks removed and cut into wedges
- 3 carrots, cut into wedges
- 1 tablespoon fresh parsley, chopped

METHOD
Put the pears and carrots through the juicer.
Stir in the chopped parsley and serve at once.

TOMATO, SPINACH AND APPLE

serves 2

INGREDIENTS
- 3 plum tomatoes, cut into wedges
- large handful of spinach leaves
- 1 apple, stalk removed and cut into wedges

METHOD
Put the tomatoes, spinach and apple through the juicer.
Stir and serve at once.

SWEET POTATO, TOMATO AND GINGER

serves 2

INGREDIENTS
- 1 large sweet potato, cut into wedges
- 3 large tomatoes, cut into wedges
- 1–2 tablespoons chopped fresh ginger

METHOD
Put the sweet potato, tomatoes and ginger through the juicer.
Stir and serve at once.

Hopefully by this stage you will be seeing fruit and vegetables in a completely new light and enjoying them more than you ever thought possible. I hope this book has inspired you to experiment with many different combinations that have led you to discover your own personal favourites.

There has been a great deal written about juicing and its benefits to health, but remember, food juices cannot be considered a miracle cure for all ailments, aches and pains. However, fresh fruit and vegetables are an important part of any balanced diet, in both their raw and cooked state, and will certainly contribute to good health and a robust immune system.

Above all, for me, as a cook and lover of food, the bottom line is that food juices not only taste fantastic but leave me feeling refreshed, invigorated and energised. So remember, next time you feel in need of a cuppa or a can of cola, reach for this book and juice up your energy!

Happy juicing!